MY LIFE FOR MY FRIENDS

ORBIS BOOKS
MARYKNOLL   NEW YORK

MY LIFE

The Guerrilla

Translated

FOR MY FRIENDS

Journal of Néstor Paz, Christian

and Edited by Ed Garcia and John Eagleson

Originally published in various sources, including *Los cristianos y la revolución,* Quimantú, Santiago de Chile, 1972, and *Suplemento de Pastoral Popular* (Santiago de Chile), no. 125

Copyright © 1975 Orbis Books, Maryknoll, New York, 10545

Library of Congress Catalog Card Number: 74-21107

ISBN: 0-88344-320-1

Manufactured in the United States of America

CONTENTS

Néstor Paz, July 15, 1970,
two days before leaving for Teoponte

Note: The photos included in My Life for My Friends
are from the Paz family album.

PUBLISHER'S
FOREWORD

This is the campaign diary of a young Bolivian university student whose name is unknown in the United States. He left his wife, his family, and a professional career to join other students in the Teoponte Campaign—a guerrilla action against his government, one of the most repressive in Latin America. That campaign was scarcely even mentioned in our news media. Vietnam, and the increasing unrest it was causing in our own universities, provided all we cared to read, see, or hear about death, devastation, or the moral dilemmas of violence versus non-violence.

The journal of Néstor Paz is short, because eighty-seven days after joining the Teoponte Campaign, Néstor Paz was dead. He did not want to die, but was prepared to die in combat. He died, instead, of starvation, only a few days before the Teoponte Campaign itself was brought to an end with ruthless efficiency by the Bolivian government forces.

Bolivia itself lost heavily in the campaign. Not the Bolivian government, which sustained little loss of either men or military equipment, but Bolivia, the nation, for Néstor Paz and his fellow guerrillas represented the best of Bolivia's university students, a spiritual nobility which felt impelled, almost in desperation, to express their patriotism as Bolivians by armed resistance to the coalition of economic privilege and military power which rules Bolivia with the velvet glove extended to the few, and the iron fist held over the many.

By birth and education, Néstor Paz and his comrades could have been among the few, but they chose to cast their lives with the cause of the many, and the iron fist crushed them. The *Journal* of Néstor Paz captures their idealism and is one of the few memorials to their courage.

His *Journal* is published, however, for reasons other than these. It might justly be titled *The Love Letters of Néstor Paz,* addressed to his family, to his young wife, to his God. These letters reflect a heroic response to what one Christian believed fidelity to the Christ of the Gospel demanded of him. One need not agree with the specific course Néstor Paz chose in order to feel moved and challenged by his witness. Thomas More did not lack family or friends to tell him he was wrong in his decision, but over four centuries even those who could not share More's convictions have been stirred by the courage with which he held them.

INTRODUCTION

Néstor Paz died of starvation on the banks of the Mariapo River on October 8, 1970, the day before his twenty-fifth birthday. He was a member of Bolivia's National Liberation Army, the ELN, and a combatant in the guerrilla campaign in the Teoponte area.

He was born on October 9, 1945, in Sucre, Bolivia. His family was neither poor nor powerless. His father was a general in the Bolivian Armed Forces and became Governor of Sucre. The Paz family was both highly respected and well liked in the town.

Néstor attended high school at the Jesuits' Colegio del Sagrado Corazón de Sucre. One of the Jesuit fathers who knew him and his family well described the boy as an intense and generous young man with an engaging manner and a confidence that was contagious. "Néstor's generous spirit and boundless confidence," he remarked, "made him stand out in school

1

and in sports. When Néstor saw a worthwhile cause he gave himself to it fully and without hesitation. He always followed his convictions to their ultimate consequences."

In 1959 Néstor entered the minor seminary, where he finished his secondary studies. In 1962 he entered the novitiate of the Redemptorist Fathers in Córdoba, Argentina. Through the mediation of the Auxiliary Bishop of La Paz, Armando Gutiérrez, he transferred to the major seminary in Santiago, Chile, where he studied from 1963 to 1966.

After leaving the seminary, he enrolled in the school of medicine at the University of San Andrés in La Paz in 1967. He dedicated much of his time to work among young people. Besides teaching religion in the Colegio Saint Andrew's, where he stressed the social demands of the faith in his classes, he also tried to organize a cooperative among the young workers in the Barrio Obrajes section. He tried to form social conscience, class consciousness, and a committed Christian spirit among the people with whom he worked. In all these efforts his constant companion was Cecilia Avila ("Cecy"), a sensitive, intelligent, and equally generous young girl whose family had known the Paz family for years. Néstor and Cecy were married on Easter Sunday, April 14, 1968.[1]

Like many other Latin American university students who share the same commitment, Néstor and Cecy strove to synthesize their Christianity with Marxist thought, particularly through prayerful reflection on the New Testament and the Psalms and careful reading of the works of Che Guevara. Néstor, for example, read the Bible daily and had great devotion to St. Francis of Assisi, the gentle saint with a consuming love for the poor. (It is significant that on joining the campaign he took "Francisco" as his battle-name, and it is as "Francisco" that he has become a symbol to many Bolivian university students and workers today.) Néstor was also deeply affected by the examples of Camilo Torres and Che Guevara. Che Guevara's vision of "the new man" and his insistence that "the true revolutionary is guided by powerful feelings of love" found resonance in Néstor. Furthermore, the experience of the Ñancahuazú campaign was a constant reminder of the price men were willing to pay for their convictions: Leading an international band of guerrilla fighters, Che Guevara together with the Peredo brothers, Inti and Coco, had hoped to initiate the revolutionary struggle on a continental scale in Bolivia; the campaign was launched from Ñancahuazú in southern Bolivia in 1966 and ended eleven months later on October 8, 1967, when Che Guevara, after being captured alive, was machine-gunned to death.

Continent of Violence

Two years before Néstor Paz joined the ranks of the Bolivian Ejército de Liberación Nacional, more than

900 priests from Mexico to Argentina addressed a document, eventually entitled "Latin America: A Continent of Violence," to the Second Conference of the Latin American Episcopate then in session in Medellín, Colombia, in August 1968.

Outstanding for its direct and perceptive analysis, the document did not hesitate to present in forceful language the insights gathered by men in close contact with the people: "For several centuries now, Latin America has been a continent of violence. The violence we are talking about is the violence that a minority of privileged people has waged against the vast majority of deprived people. It is the violence of hunger, helplessness, and underdevelopment. It is the violence of persecution, oppression, and neglect." Together with this basic understanding of what in the first place constitutes the reality of violence, the text pointed out the emergence of a new factor on the continent: "For some time now, however, a new element has been taking shape in this panorama of poverty and injustice. It is the rapid and growing self-awareness of the exploited peoples, who see a real possibility for their own liberation. For many this liberation is impossible without a fundamental change in the socio-economic structures of our continent . . . . Because the privileged few use their power of repression to block this process of liberation, many see the use of force as the only solution open to the people. This same conclusion is being reached by many militant Christians whose own lives faithfully reflect the light of the Gospel."[2]

The document concludes with a set of recommendations which are extremely important for appreciating the thinking on the problem of violence in Latin America and elsewhere in the Third World. First, the basic difference between the unjust violence of the oppressors and the just violence of the oppressed is unequivocally stated. It is not right to equate indiscriminately what is so blatantly inhuman and deliberately maintained with what is so evidently a response of a people who find themselves driven to violence in their effort to achieve liberation. Second, while affirming the right of the people to legitimate defense, the 900 priests also recognized the need to denounce the state of violence perpetrated by powerful individuals, groups, or nations over the vast majority who are voiceless and poor.

Finally, the Latin American priests encourage the efforts of Christians sincerely searching for paths leading to authentic liberation on the continent. Ground must be broken in the search for a just and fraternal society. They ask that the Church respect the consciences of people genuinely groping for ways to bring about an authentic liberation process. "Let us accord these Christians," the document concludes, "a broader margin of liberty in choosing the means they deem most suitable for obtaining liberation and building such a society."

Spiral of Violence

Describing the situation of violence in Latin America, Archbishop Dom Helder Camara, the prophetic voice from the Brazilian Northeast, perceptively analyzes the phenomenon as a "spiral of violence."[3] He interrelates and further defines the three forms of violence which the 900 priests had forcefully confronted. "Institutionalized violence" is the term he employs to describe the basic situation of injustice and oppression which the foreign economic powers and their native counterparts perpetuate in the dependent countries of Latin America. Increasingly, so-called independent republics find their economies and socio-political life dominated by the dictates of foreign interest and the native ruling oligarchy, who together subtly exercise a form of external and internal neo-colonialism on the majority of the people.

To break this exploitative stranglehold, people and movements on the continent have responded with counter-violence. This violence-in-response, manifested in dramatic fashion in Castro's revolution in Cuba and in the brave but tragic attempts at armed struggle to achieve liberation in Guatemala, Venezuela, Colombia, Uruguay, Brazil, Peru, and Bolivia, further found incarnation in the examples of Camilo Torres in Colombia and Che Guevara and Néstor Paz in Bolivia.

Finally, a third form of violence in the escalating

"spiral" is unleashed by the repressive forces of the State and the regimes serving the interests of the ruling few. This repressive violence finds concrete expression in the military dictatorships which do not hesitate to use their might mercilessly, engaging in arbitrary arrests, government-instigated kidnappings and killings, imprisonment, and torture. In a 224-page Amnesty International Report on Torture published in December 1973, for example, the widespread existence of torture in Latin America is sadly acknowledged: "Costa Rica is the only country in Latin America from which Amnesty International has received no torture allegations of any kind within the past year."[4]

Bolivia's Tragic History

In Bolivia the "spiral of violence" has always been part of its tragic history. Centrally located in the Andean heartland of Latin America, Bolivia shares frontiers with Brazil, Peru, Chile, Argentina, and Paraguay. Its five million people have a long heritage of struggle. It was the first Latin American country to revolt against Spain, with the declaration of Chuquisaca in 1809. After fifteen years of armed struggle, the Republic of Bolivia was born with Simón Bolívar leading the truimphal march of the Latin American army into La Paz. Bolivia has had a turbulent history since then. Land-locked as a result of the loss of its access to the ocean in the "War of the Pacific" against Chile and Peru (1879), Bolivia was further humiliated by its de-

7

feat in the "War of the Chaco" against Paraguay (1932). Celebrating 150 years of existence as an independent republic on August 6, 1975, Bolivia also has to acknowledge the 188 military coups, or *golpes de estado,* it has so far experienced in its history.[5]

Years before the Cuban socialist revolution, a significant social upheaval took place in Bolivia with resounding repercussions for the whole continent. In 1952 the tin miners of the Siglo XX and Catavi mines, among the most combative working-class group in Latin America, battled to usher in a government pledged to nationalize mining enterprises and initiate land reform; hopes were high that a social restructuring was to take place in earnest. But as far as "La Rosca" (the Bolivian tin oligarchy—composed of the family interests of Patiño, Hoschild, and Aramayo—, the big landowners, and the traditional ruling elite) was concerned, the reforms showed signs of an unwanted social revolution.[6] The shifting strategies of international capital and multinational businesses, combined with the staying power of the well-entrenched native mining and land oligarchs in collaboration with the state bureaucracy and the armed forces, largely reversed popular gains. In 1964 "La Rosca" installed a repressive regime under the dictatorship of Gen. René Barrientos.

In 1967 the Ñancahuazú guerrilla campaign took place, leading to the death of Che Guevara and shaking the complacency of the continent. The lessons of

8

Ñancahuazú were not lost on the youth and workers of Bolivia: The guns of the guerrillas did not create the violence; the violence was generated by the system responsible for the criminal poverty and the endless injustice, the open or camouflaged unemployment and underemployment of the majority of Bolivians, the lack of medical attention (five out of every ten Bolivians do not receive medical care), the illiteracy among the peasant population who represent more than 70 percent of the nation and live and die without basic social rights, the national anomaly that at birth every Bolivian inherits a public debt of 1,200 pesos because of the nation's massive foreign debt.[7]

Teoponte

When the ELN launched the Teoponte Campaign in 1970, the socio-political situation in Bolivia was both complex and ambiguous. Gen. Alfredo Ovando was head of the military regime which had seized power after the *golpe de estado* of September 1969. Ovando's regime was a self-styled "revolutionary national model of development" and differentiated itself from the socialist model. In a move designed to co-opt nationalist sectors of the population, the regime nationalized Bolivian Gulf Oil, paying some $78.6 million as indemnization.

"Volvimos a las montañas" ("We Have Returned to the Mountains"), the ideological platform drafted in

1970 by the high command of the ELN to announce the renewal of the armed phase of the struggle for liberation in Bolivia, signaled the need for a socialist revolution that would be basically anti-imperialist. It enumerated by name some twenty-four multinational corporations that had thoroughly penetrated Bolivian economic life and made profits at criminal rates. The high command also singled out strategic sectors of industry held by foreign interests: mining, transportation, communications, petroleum and gas, rubber, liquor and tobacco, importation of basic machinery, banking operations, and others.[8] They denounced Ovando's proclamation of his regime as a "revolutionary nationalist" government to be both deceptive and dishonest. As a response to the situation, the men of the ELN chose the path of armed struggle and the opening of the guerrilla front with two basic objectives: to produce a deep political impact and to accentuate the weaknesses of the military.[9] They also underscored one of their basic tasks: "To achieve a progressive *concientización* [raising of political consciousness] of the people by means of example and concrete deeds. Only in this way can the people achieve a political formation and be transformed into the unique protagonists of the revolution."[10]

Although Teoponte ended in death and defeat 87 days after the ELN militants entered the combat zone, their limited objectives were largely achieved. There were, of course, tragic mistakes in political analysis and shortcomings in their perception of socio-political realities. In an effort of self-criticism, the survivors of Teoponte themselves evaluated their own experience and emphasized the following points as crucial factors in their defeat: the lack of sufficient preparatory political work among the people in the zone chosen for the guerrilla campaign, the lack of sufficient care in the selection and training of the combatants for the armed phase of the struggle, the inevitable geographical isolation that resulted from a lack of urban support and a base among the people in urban centers and rural areas, the inexperience of the high command, and the insufficient political and military preparation of the cadres.

Two other brief observations might be added. First, during the early seventies the Bolivian socio-political scene was extremely fluid, complex, and nuanced, making it difficult for any group to enunciate a comprehensive political strategy.[11] In this regard, the ELN's choice of a politico-military tactical weapon such as the *foco guerrillero* (expanding center of rural guerrilla activity) did not have a well-prepared, long-range political strategy to back up its armed operations. Second, while lacking a sufficiently strong base of active support among the population, the ELN underestimated the repressive power of the military apparatus unleashed against them, which progressively gained in efficiency and brutality. Teoponte, then, is once again a demonstration of the "spiral of violence."

Testament of Love

"Francisco" died three years to the day after Che Guevara. The official files of the ELN which contained the names of the combatants and the casualties briefly recorded: "Néstor Paz Zamora ("Francisco"). Ex-seminarian. Religion teacher. Bolivian. Died of starvation. An example of daily heroism and love for man. His struggle to become the 'new man' whom Che Guevara sought is an example for all revolutionaries."

Omar (Jorge Gustavo Ruíz Paz), Francisco's cousin and fellow guerrilla, reported that "Néstor shared his thoughts with us during the reflections and discussions we had every night. He made us see new dimensions to the struggle. He made us realize that we had to see something more and that we had to look beyond today and tomorrow." It was perhaps for this reason that the officers of the Armed Forces who attacked the guerrilla column stated that according to their intelligence reports "there was a priest" in the column.

The Campaign Journal of Francisco is a testament of love lived today in the Third World. A careful reading of the entries in his diary shows a profound integration of the loves in his life: his love for God, for his people, for his companions, for his family, and for his wife. Love, if it is real and concrete, is one and whole. Francisco met his God among his people. His beautiful and sensitive love for his wife was possible because of the bedrock experience of God's steadfast love in his

12

life. In Francisco's words, "God is here and I feel his presence." It was an all-pervasive sense of God in the here-and-now, in the historical present, that made possible his commitment, his consistent selflessness, and his ultimate, unhesitating self-gift.

The life and death of Néstor Paz deepens our realization that the basic evangelical challenge to love is not simply a word to be spoken but a life to be lived.

The Campaign Journal is, then, more than just an extraordinary document of a revolutionary engaged in armed struggle. For anyone who reads the moving account with openness and honesty, the Campaign Journal poses an unsettling challenge—a challenge which questions the direction of one's life and the worth of one's cause. Because Néstor Paz speaks with his life, and because his message is written in blood, his message cannot be ignored.

Francisco's death was an irrefutable proof of his love. His death by hunger has become a symbol of the cause he fought for: so to live that no one need any longer experience hunger for food, for justice, or for that liberation which is at the heart of the Gospel.

Ed Garcia
Cuernavaca, Mexico

1. Cecilia was later killed by the gunfire of Bolivian troopers during the repression of student militants and miners under the Banzer regime. She died in Cochabamba on March 23, 1972, while trying to protect people in an underground house of the ELN.

2. "Latin America: A Continent of Violence," in *Between Honesty and Hope*, trans. John Drury (Maryknoll, N.Y.: Maryknoll Publications, 1970).

3. Helder Camara, *Espiral de violencia* (Salamanca: Sígueme, 1970).

4. *Amnesty International Report on Torture* (London: Duckworth, 1973), p.178.

5. *Chile, Peru, Bolivia: Documentos de tres procesos latinoamericanos*, introduction and selection by Hugo M. Sacchi (Buenos Aires: Centro Editor de América Latina, 1972), pp. 171-73. For a more comprehensive general treatment of Bolivia, see L. Valerie Fifer, *Bolivia: Land, Location and Politics since 1825* (London: Cambridge University Press, 1972).

6. A classic work on the Bolivian tin oligarchy and "La Rosca" is Sergio Almaraz's *Requiem para una república* (Cochabamba: Los Amigos del Libro, 1967). See also Charles F. Geddes, *Patino: The Tin King* (London: Robert Hale, 1972). For a critical analysis of the 1952 Bolivian Revolution, see Guillermo Lora, *La revolución boliviana: análisis crítico* (La Paz: Difusión, 1963). See also James Malloy and Richard Thorn, eds., *Beyond the Revolution: Bolivia since 1952* (Pittsburgh: Pittsburgh University Press, 1971) and James Malloy, *Bolivia: The Uncompleted Revolution* (Pittsburgh: Pittsburgh University Press, 1970).

7. See "Mensaje al pueblo boliviano," III Encuentro nacional de ISAL, in *Signos de liberación* (Lima: CEP, 1973), pp. 208-11.

8. See the well-researched NACLA documentation on the contribution of U.S. private investment to underdevelopment in Latin America: *Yanqui Dollar*, ed. North American Congress on Latin America, 1971.

9. "Conclusiones de la etapa guerrillera," from the ELN pamphlet, *Teoponte, Nuestra experiencia guerrillera*, a document included in *Teoponte: Experiencia guerrillera boliviana*, ed. Hugo Assmann (Caracas: Editorial C. M. Nueva Izquierda, 1971).

10. "Volvimos a las montañas, plataforma ideológica de la guerrilla," in *Teoponte: Experiencia guerrillera boliviana*, p. 44.

14

11. To get a feel for the Bolivian socio-political situation at this time, see the excellent weekly political and economic report, *Latin America,* published by Latin American Newsletters, Ltd., in London (U.S. representative: William Holub, 432 Park Avenue South, New York, N.Y. 10016). See especially vols. 4 and 5, which cover the events of 1970 and 1971. For coverage of the coups and counter-coups and the other political events which took place in rapid succession before and after Teoponte, see the following: René Zavaleta Mercado, *Por qué cayó Bolivia en manos del fascismo* (Santiago: Punto Final, 1972); José Luis Alcázar and José Baldivia, *Bolivia ¿El Vietnam que anunció el Che?* (Santiago: Prensa Latinoamericana, 1971); Jorge Gallardo Lozada, *De Torres a Banzer: Diez meses de emergencia en Bolivia* (Buenos Aires: Ediciones Periferia, 1972).

Néstor's wife "Cecy" (Cecilia Avila de Paz), April 14, 1967, the year she first met Néstor

TO LOVE IS TO DIE
FOR YOUR FRIENDS

(The last poem of Néstor Paz)

To be poured into old wineskins
to cease being
to weep for being
to be other
to be silent
solitary tree, hand on the landscape
we are winepresses of the memory,
life clarifying in the joy of being.
Who would say that we must learn to love?
Whoever would say that to love
is to die.
Felled cedar
alcoholic green and wasted

17

to die for your friends
wood for the sated's fire,
to die for your friends
crackling struggle
twitching hand
emptiness of being.
To die for your friends
to fill your hands
not to dry your tears
cease the mourning
litany of selfgiving.
To die for your friends
to die in oblivion
to die for your friends.
Oh, my beloved of the dusty roads,
so many dreams
so many hands interwoven
with songs sweet to the ear;
oh, beloved, companion of the dawn.
Who would say that we must learn to love,
that to love is to die for your friends.
Subworld of the mediocre,
a lawn, a pleasant lawn,
and the bank account,
and the life insurance,
and the world of competition,
and to die for your friends
for the alienation

that gallops through your veins,
to die for your friends,
to forget the last name,
the smell, the color,
of the competition of the status money quo.
To give your life for your friends
and to learn to love.
To die in oblivion
announced today
Thursday night
comfort tomorrow
Friday afternoon.
To transcend in wheatgrain,
to be ground up for bread,
to dry the tears.
No more weeping!
To be able to see the people
with hope-filled eyes,
to be able to say
get set to be a man,
to be a man
to be other,
extended hand
loving cedar
love-man-love.

Néstor's mother and two sisters,
Rosario and Edicita, 1969

MESSAGE OF NESTOR PAZ
ON LEAVING TO JOIN
THE GUERRILLAS IN TEOPONTE,
July 17, 1970

"Every sincere revolutionary must realize that armed struggle is the only path that remains" (Camilo Torres, January 7, 1966).[1]

Following the glorious path taken by our own heroes, the guerrillas of the Peruvian highlands, and by the continental heroes, Bolívar and Sucre, and the heroic commitment of Ernesto Guevara, the Peredo brothers, Darío,[2] and many others who lead the march of the people's liberation, we take our place in the long guerrilla file, rifle in hand, to combat the symbol and instrument of oppression—the "gorilla" army.[3]

As long as blood flows in our veins we will make heard the cutting cry of the exploited. Our lives do not matter if we can make our Latin America, *la patria grande*, a free territory of free people who are masters of their own destiny.

I realize that my decision and that of my companions will bring upon us a deluge of accusations, from the paternalistic "poor misguided fellow," to the open charge of "demagogic criminal." But Yahweh our God, the Christ of the Gospels, has announced the "good news of the liberation of man," for which he himself acted. We cannot sit and spend long hours reading the Gospel with cardinals, bishops, and pastors, all of whom are doing fine right where they are, while the flock wanders about in hunger and solitude. Doing this is called "non-violence," "peace," "Gospel." These persons, sadly, are today's Pharisees.

People no longer listen to the "Good News." Man is always betrayed by his "brother."

"Peace" is not something one finds by chance; it is the result of equality among people, as Isaiah says in his chapter 58. Peace is the result of love among people, the result of an end to exploitation.

"Peace" is not attained by dressing up in silk and living in a medieval palace, or by robbing the people in order to have a millionaire's salary, or by playing on the people's religious superstition in order to live at their expense.

"Greater love than this no man has than to lay down his life for his friends." This is the commandment which sums up the "Law."

For this reason we have taken up arms: to defend the

unlettered and undernourished majority from the exploitation of a minority and to win back dignity for a dehumanized people.

We know that violence is painful because we feel in our own flesh the violent repression of the established disorder. But we are determined to liberate man because we consider *him a brother*. We are the people in arms. This is the only path that remains. Man comes before the "Sabbath," not vice versa.

They say violence is not evangelical; let them remember Yahweh slaying the first-born of the Egyptians to free his people from exploitation.

They say that they believe in "non-violence." Then let them stand clearly with the people. If they do, the rich and the "gorillas" will both demand their lives, just as they demanded Christ's. Let them take courage and try it; let us see if they are consistent enough to face a Good Friday. But all that is demagoguery, isn't it, you canons, generals, *cursillistas*,[4] priests of the established disorder, you priests of the peace enforced by violence, of the massacre of San Juan,[5] of the complicity of silence, of the 200-peso salaries, of the widespread tuberculosis, and of pie in the sky when you die. The Gospel is not mechanical moralism. It is a shell hiding a "life" which must be discovered if we are not to fall into pharisaism. The Gospel is "Jesus among us."

We have chosen this path because it is the only path left open to us, painful though it may be.

Fortunately, there are some, and their numbers are growing, who recognize the authenticity of our position and who either help us or have joined our ranks. We need only consider what the right-wing "gorilla" government of Brazil does to a committed Church: Father Pereira Neto was assassinated in a most cruel and inhuman manner.[6] Or recall Father Ildefonso, a Tupamaro, assassinated in Uruguay. Or Father Camilo Torres, silenced by the government and the servile church. But Camilo Torres ratified with his blood what he had said about Christianity:

> In Catholicism the main thing is love for one's fellow men: " . . . He who loves his fellow man has fulfilled the Law." For this love to be genuine, it must seek to be effective. If works of beneficence, almsgiving, the few tuition-free schools, the few housing projects —everything which is known as "charity"—do not succeed in feeding the majority of the hungry, in clothing the majority of the naked, or in teaching the majority of the ignorant, then we must seek effective means to achieve the well-being of this majority . . . . This is why the revolution is not only permissible but obligatory for those Christians who see it as the only effective and far-reaching way to make love for all people a reality.[7]

I believe that taking up arms is the only effective way of protecting the poor against their present exploitation, the only effective way of generating a free man.

I believe that the struggle for liberation is rooted in the prophetic line of Salvation History.

Enough of the languid faces of the over-pious! The whip of justice, so often betrayed by elegant gentlemen, will fall on the exploiter, that false Christian who forgets that the force of his Lord ought to drive him to liberate his neighbor from sin, that is to say, from every lack of love.

We believe in a "New Man," made free by the blood and resurrection of Jesus. We believe in a New Earth, where love will be the fundamental law. This will come about, however, only by breaking the old patterns based on selfishness. We don't want patches. New cloth can't be used to mend old garments, nor can new wine be put into old wineskins. Conversion implies first an inner violence which is then followed by violence against the exploiter. May both men and the Lord together judge the rightness of our decision. At least no one can imply that we look for profit or comfort. These are not what we find in the struggle; they are what we leave behind.

The Lord said, "He who loves father or mother more than me is not worthy of me, and he who loves son or daughter more than me is not worthy of me" (Matthew), and "He who does not hate even his own life cannot be my disciple" (Luke). We believe that the Lord is referring to the person tied to his "own little world" and his "own little problems." The "other person" is out there beyond our "own comfort."

There are those who defend themselves with lyrical discourses about the "revolution"; yet at the moment

25

of truth, because of their cowardice, they take the side of the oppressor. The sin of "omission" is the fault of our Church, just as it was of the "lukewarm" members (Rev. 3:14–22), just as it is of those who do not want "to get their hands dirty." We don't want to bequeath to our children a vision of life based upon competition as a means of possession, or on possessions as a measure of man's value.

We believe in a man who has value for who he is, and not for what he has. We believe in a completely liberated man who will live and build brotherly structures through which love may be expressed.

I am certain that we can achieve this goal, for the Lord "is ready to give us far more than all we can ask or think" (Ephesians 3:20).

"The duty of every Christian is to be a revolutionary. The duty of every revolutionary is to bring about the revolution."[8]

Victory or Death.

Francisco

1. Camilo Torres, a Colombian priest and sociologist, university chaplain and editor of *Frente Unido*, joined the Colombian National Liberation Army and explained the reasons for this decision in "A Message to Colombians from the Mountains" on January 7, 1966. A month later he was killed in an encounter with a national army patrol. The example and writings of Camilo Torres had a deep impact on Néstor Paz. See *Revolutionary Priest: The Complete Writings and Messages of Camilo Torres*, ed. John Gerassi (New York: Vintage, 1971).

2. Inti and Coco Peredo as well as "Darío" (Arturo Alvarado Durán) were combatants in Che Guevara's Bolivian campaign.

3. "Gorilla" refers to reactionary military forces.

4. The *cursillo* is a renewal movement of Spanish origin geared toward deepening the commitment of lay Catholics. In Bolivia its composition is largely from the middle and affluent classes and it has come to be identified with a conservative or reactionary orientation.

5. Massacre of miners and their families in the mining centers of Siglo XX and Catavi perpetrated by Bolivian soldiers on St. John the Baptist's Day, June 24, 1967. The massacre was ordered by then President René Barrientos, who feared the solidarity of the miners with the forces of Che Guevara. The date is widely commemorated among oppositon forces in Bolivia today.

6. Henrique Pereira Neto, a university chaplain in Recife, Brazil, was an assistant to Archbishop Dom Helder Camara, world renowned champion of the poor and oppressed. Father Pereira Neto was kidnapped, tortured, and killed by para-military right-wing forces in Brazil in May 1969.

7. Camilo Torres, "Message to Christians," published in *Frente Unido*, August 26, 1965.

8. Ibid.

27

Néstor and his mother, Mrs. Edith Zamora de Paz,
April 14, 1968, at Néstor and Cecy's wedding

A FAREWELL LETTER
TO HIS PARENTS

July 17, 1970
La Paz, 1 A.M.

My beloved parents,

I write these lines to say goodbye, for we are leaving early in the morning. I taped a message for Cecy, and in it I also have something for you. Mario[1] will bring it to you.

At this moment I am happy, for I realize that I am achieving the goal of my life: to do something meaningful for others, to put into concrete actions my desire to love. On the other hand, I am also sad because I have to be physically far away from those I love the most.

I am at the end of my search, and now it is simply a matter of realizing my dream, God willing.

A big warm hug, a loving kiss for you both. Today I

received Christ in communion, perhaps for the last time. I have an unbreakable faith in the decision that I have made because I am convinced that it is the path of the Lord.

Goodbye. If death surprises me, I will wait for you in the New Land, loving without fail. Kisses for you and my sisters.

Victory or Death.

Francisco

---

1. Néstor's older brother and a surgeon in La Paz.

THE CAMPAIGN JOURNAL
OF NESTOR PAZ

During the Teoponte Campaign, Néstor Paz carried a small, black notebook. In the tradition of Che Guevara, whose diary entries during the 1967 Ñancahuazú campaign were later read by militants around the world, the Bolivian ELN had several of their members keeping journals during the Teoponte Campaign. As far as the friends and family of Néstor Paz know, we have the complete edition of the journal written by him. In the original it seems that three pages had been torn out when the family received the journal. It is thought that these pages contained Néstor's personal critique and evaluation of the technical, politico-military aspects of the campaign. For internal security reasons a member of the ELN apparently kept these pages.

My dear princess,[1]

I'm sitting at the foot of a very steep sandstone hill waiting for the minutes to pass by before suppertime.

Yesterday marked our first week in this new life. First of all, I want to tell you I've missed you as part of my being, my very substance. Things are going well in spite of the fact that we have in the same band seventy different individuals.[2]

I'm going to play cards. I'll be back soon.

There was no card game, but I spent the time talking to Choco. He's completely discouraged and can't take it anymore. I tried to encourage him. I think I helped a little. Our biggest problem is to feel that we are protected by our comrades and closely related to them.

When we left Teoponte I was terribly sad. I began needing you. In this place I didn't find the one I love, the one who has never let me down—and this made me panicky, afraid.

We are getting ourselves together as a group, and this is the most difficult stage. Yesterday we went down to a poor town to buy a few things. We are behind the town of Guanay. We talked with some peasants who were friendly enough and willing to lend us a hand. Our feast of pork was good, with some bananas and yucca. Today, I think, we'll eat roasted corn. We miss food a lot, and the most wretched morsel seems like a great delicacy.

I am well, and things are beginning to take shape. Yesterday two of our men got lost. I prayed for them. Today they found their way back.

I hope my ability to love continues to grow at the same rate as my ability as a guerrilla fighter. It is the only way of qualitatively improving the revolutionary spirit.

I think of you a lot and I love you.

---

1. Néstor addresses most of the entries in his campaign journal to his wife Cecilia, whom he calls "Cecy," *Reina adorada, Querida reinita, Amorcito*, and other affectionate names.

2. The ELN's official list of combatants put the number at 67 (see *Presencia*, January 16, 1971). Father Jaime Zalles, a member of the Peace Commission which mediated between the government and the last surviving members of the ELN in Teoponte, confirmed this figure, while in *Teoponte: Experiencia guerrillera boliviana*, Hugo Assmann puts the number at 75.

I'm taking advantage of this rest period to write you. We're doing fine. I think of nothing but you. I'm beginning to pray with a basis and a foundation, and this unites me with everything that is ours, besides providing me with the dimension of the Lord Jesus.

Yesterday eight men left us, the first ones to crack. One of them was Choco. I gave him some things for you in case he gets the chance to give them to you. I especially asked him to encourage you to keep on going, because this is the most practical way of expressing our love for each other. I asked him to tell you that I am strong and loving you more every day.

The column is being purified to a great extent, although I think that more will be leaving. We have not clashed with the army, but we are about to. We've learned about Ovando's son.[1]

The words in that *zamba* song are true: "Everything I look at, we've already seen together." Everything here reminds me of you—everything you've prepared for me with so much affection. All my equipment is complete, thanks to you. I have everything I need.

I have great confidence in the coming victory and in the ability of the men to achieve it, although I doubt that many of us will see it.

I miss you and I love you totally. I never thought we could be so together as we are now. To become as one.

35

Anyhow, we've done all we could, don't you think? Even if I die, I know that I'm one with you. The Resurrection now has a real meaning in my life, and it is no longer just a "truth." I want to grow in depth and penetrate more profoundly into "life" and "man." I want to reach the point of total humanization. This is the vocation of my life and definitely our fulfillment.

My closest companions are those of the first squad of the vanguard. They are excellent men, and almost all of us have learned to get along well together.

Yesterday we had a delicious meal and ate like mad. It's funny how every bite has an "inexhaustible" worth. We're on to "something" here. We've stopped the march.

---

1. Marcelo Ovando, 21 year-old son of General Alfredo Ovando, then head of the Bolivian military regime. On the return from a reconnaissance flight over the Teoponte guerrilla zone, the military plane in which he was flying accidentally crashed near Lake Titicaca on July 29, 1970.

Today is "the day,"[1] right, princess? One more anniversary. I remember you with a special affection. I love you.

I had two difficult days before yesterday. We had two favorable encounters with the army, but I had to revise my whole way of thinking. It probably had to do with the violence, the commitment, the meaning of the struggle, the value of a sacrifice, the effectiveness of our troops, etc., and at the root of all this, your absence. I thought about it, and it made me bitter. But I grew. It was really hard to leave behind the model of the "old man" and exchange it for the model of a "new man." All growth means pain, and this is what I felt. Growth also means not being sure if these are the paths of the Lord. But today I am more at peace, more calm, and I've made a resolution that I'm determined to keep:

First, I am in this struggle until victory or death.

Second, this is the path on which history advances; there is no other.

Third, if this is so, then this is Christian, especially if we keep in mind the prophetic role of Camilo Torres.

Fourth, being here I am more fully with you because we are fulfilling the ideal of our lives.

I remember you once again and the parties at Muda García's place, the motorcycle, the Sunday mornings,

our first kiss, every happy moment we spent together
—and the tragic ones too. I better not keep thinking
about all these things because it makes me want to be
by your side, and that is not bad.

Things are going well. We've already gone through
our baptism of fire. The prospects are excellent, and
only our own shortcomings and weakness can make
them change. These first three months are decisive.
Afterward I think everything will go better. I have
begun praying with more fulness and confidence.

Well, I'll leave you for now. I love you. Oh, by the
way, I lost my cap with the cross on it and the handkerchief with the words "Everything and always." You'll
make me a new one, won't you?

---

1. August 1 commemorates Néstor and Cecy's first meeting at
the Universidad de San Andrés in La Paz, where he was studying
medicine and she was studying biochemistry.

We've started the march, and it's already 10:30 A.M. The men are very tired, and I think it's because we don't have any good food. Our main dish every day is one or two spoonfuls of boiled rice with salt. Sometimes we have dried meat, sometimes we don't. This is making us very weak. I'm already feeling some pain and fatigue in my legs. Other than this, my body has served me well.

It seems that the eight men who left us the other day were killed. They were not armed and were killed in cold blood. Before he left, Choco left me the photo which we had taken together in San Pedro.

That's how things are going. We are looking for sources of supplies and ways to strike at the army.

Yesterday all of us who had not done it before swore an oath before a picture of Che Guevara. It will be a day of double memories for me—a double pledge of love for you and love for the revolution. Deep down they are the same thing.

We've been apart for two weeks, and today I was looking again at your picture and your little note. What you tell me is so incredibly beautiful that I get a lump in my throat every time I read it. I love you. I hope the time flies by so that I can see you or at least get to some place where I can hear some news from you. For now, I trust that you are well. I can imagine how worried you all must be, the folks and Mario and Jaime,[1] etc. What bothers me most is that I can't be in touch with all of you. But I better not keep on thinking of these things because it just makes matters worse. We have come to a beautiful sandstone mountain and a quiet woods, dry and filled with small sweet fruits. It was our Sunday walk. I thought of you and how nice it would be to take a walk here with you.

––––––––––

1. Mario is the eldest of the Paz family (see above, "A Farewell Letter to his Parents," note 1). Jaime, like Néstor, studied in the seminary; later he went to Louvain, Belgium, to study sociology and is now a militant member of the Bolivian resistance. Néstor was the third child. The two youngest are Rosario and Edicita.

How are things, princess? Midday. 1:15. Listening to Radio Altiplano.[1] Things are going fine, although we're a little hungry. We're entering a different type of mountain zone. It's lower, dry and pleasant, with possibilities for hunting. This morning we caught two big, beautiful monkeys, so tonight we'll have a banquet. It will be a welcome treat. In a few days we'll be having the national holidays.[2]

So, I leave you now, and I love you. I hope to hear from you soon.

The knapsack is heavy, and we are already a little weak.

---

1. Radio Altiplano has one of the most powerful transmitters in Bolivia. It regularly broadcasts news and is widely listened to.

2. August 6 is Bolivia's Independence Day.

We're about to leave the campsite. It's quarter to seven. There's a long day ahead of us. We're going to gather provisions, since we're a little low on food. Last night we had monkey "stew." It was delicious. Too bad it didn't last long.

As the days go by we are little by little becoming better prepared. We know what we'll have to face in the days to come, and this is a perfect novitiate. We have already learned more or less how to adjust our bodies to this new world and to the tasks at hand. The morale of the men is high, but the lack of food makes them weak and very tired. Anyhow, it's not the first time nor the last that we'll be in tight situations. The people who lived with us—except for Choco who didn't make the grade and seems to have been killed—all have come out determined and in high spirits, and we're getting along well together.[1]

We're eating a lot of wild fruits, and they're tasty. And also a kind of mushroom called "monkey's ear" that's very good. The *palmito* plant has also helped us out, and it's good besides.

I keep trying to penetrate more into the reality of "God, man, and history." Maybe I can write you more on this in the next few days. I pray easily, but it's like the stutterings of a beginner. God is here and I feel him. The Psalms give me a lot of strength.

I don't have to tell you that I'm always thinking of you. I love you and I need you. I just hope we can see each other soon. Please God.

I think today is María del Carmen's birthday. I'm sending her a kiss from far away. She is a sister I love very much. I imagine that in a ''limited'' way you must spend some time with them.[2]

---

1. The Bolivian ELN in Teoponte was composed of various groups who joined the guerrilla campaign convinced that armed struggle was one effective means to bring about social justice. Néstor Paz led one group of five referred to here, who were members of a Christian reflection and action group somewhat like a *comunidad cristiana de base* (Christian base community). One of the incidents which radicalized Néstor Paz's group was the ''prom protest,'' which they held in front of the Hotel La Paz, where a luxurious debut party was going on. To call attention to the glaring social inequalities existent in Bolivian society, Néstor's *grupo de convivencia cristiana* picketed the party. Someone inside the hotel threw a bomb at the protestors, killing one of them, Juan Poma, a student at the Jesuit college of San Calixto. This incident, which occurred almost a year before Teoponte, deeply affected Néstor and his companions.

2. María del Carmen is the wife of Néstor's brother Mario. Néstor rightly thought that his brother's home would be watched by the military police after Néstor left for Teoponte. What he did not know was that Cecy had slipped into his brother's house before the military could set up their vigilance and was hiding out there.

We're marching toward a new campsite. It's 8 A.M., and we've stopped for the briefing. Things are going fine, and I've adjusted well to this new reality. Last night we had an invigorating supper of rice with dried meat and *palmitos*, and this has given us strength for the journey. I feel good today. The men are in high spirits, and we expect to gather supplies so we can strike when and where we want. From the radio reports it seems that the situation in La Paz has become tense. The internal division within their army has helped us immensely, even if it's only to give us a breather.[1] I think that the column is winding up its training. Now we know what it is to carry a load, what everything is worth here, especially what kind of food we need the most, what a clash with the enemy is, what a little hunger and weakness means.

There has been a marked improvement among the men. They are beginning to have a sense of brotherhood. All this is essential for our future action: it's the infrastructure of the column.

Yesterday I was thinking about all of you and especially about María del Carmen. I've hoped that the quality of the home situation has improved a lot, although recently it seemed to me that things have been going very well. I try to imagine your daily chores. I guess you're working on gear for the troops and other little things. You'll end up by being a perfect seamstress so that all our little Pazes[2] will never have to go to the store. Their mamma will fit them out like beautiful guerrilla models.

---

1. The governmental and military crisis was coming to a head at about the same time as the ELN forces were gathering in Teoponte. In July 1970 General Juan José Torres was relieved of his post as Commander-in-Chief of the Army by the military president, General Ovando. On August 3, police agents of the Ministry of the Interior tried to arrest General Torres. The La Paz newspaper *Prensa* accused the new Commander-in-Chief of the Army, General Rogelio Miranda, of preparing another coup against Ovando. This actually took place sometime later when, on October 5, Miranda proclaimed himself head of a new governing military junta. In a quick countermove, the forces led by General Torres fought back and won victory on October 7 to usher in a short-lived, nationalist orientated government that was overthrown by rightist forces led by Colonel Hugo Banzer on August 21, 1971.

2. Spanish: "Pazuelopis."

We're "hibernating" in the campsite. Today I'll try to study the Gospel and the Psalms. I'm well, my dear princess, except that I miss you so much I could die. I love you. It's not "sentimental gush," but something concrete, real, vital. I'll tell you again that I realize perfectly well how deeply you've become a part of me, that is, if you haven't actually become fully one with me. I'm sure you have the same feeling.

We are beginning the take-off stage. No matter what happens, we'll rise up. We're in the course of history, of truth. The Lord is showing his face, or rather, we are weaving it with the threads which reality gives us and we ourselves create.

I think that all this abundance of energy, feeling, and desire in this group of men can make at least a little crack in this closed-off reality in which we are prisoners. This better world that we dream of will be a reality to the degree that we are faithful to its call. There is a desperate cry which by our cowardice we have often ignored or directly silenced. Out here we are experiencing all that this means. Of this I'm sure: Our children will live in a better world.

We will have fulfilled the commandment, "Greater love no man has than to lay down his life for his friends." I have been reading some passages from Mayol.[1] It's really a summary of all this, and an

46

ideological stimulus. In a very real way we have recently felt pulled by constructive forces and destructive ones, by love and the lack of love. This produces a double process: First, from outside, or the clash with the world which we fight; second, from within, or with the unceasing conversion to love, to an abandonment of everything that is "ours."

The details are the most painful part, especially those having to do with food and sharing with others life's little treasures like cigarettes, candy, tobacco, or little household articles. It's a constant struggle between faithfulness to the "great" challenge, that is, the struggle against the structure, and the "little" challenges, in other words, against our own interior personal and communal structure. It's a totally interrelated dialectical movement. It's clear to me now that, although we saw this clearly "there," "here" it takes on all its real dimensions.

Personal conscious faith and the faith of all our comrades who, even if they don't believe, are "on the road," meet in the loving arms of the Lord. If it is a real encounter, even a mystical one because it is vital, it is becoming continuously more perfect. "The Lord is my Shepherd, nothing shall I want." How true this is.

"My soul waits for the Lord more than the watchman waits for the dawn." It is a desire for encounter with the Absolute, for destroying everything that can separate us so that we can get at the heart of the "matter," where the ferment of the "real," of what "is," of the "Absolute," is in turmoil.

You are here with me, infinitely present, because we are touching the root of what we are and what we want to become. This movement from love to faith and from faith to hope returning again to love becomes a concrete reality.

I'm by the coals of our breakfast fire drying my socks and my bathing suit. Yesterday, for the first time in eighteen days, I took a bath and disinfected myself, changed my socks and washed what I could. In doing all these things I remembered your very sensible suggestions.

---

1. Alejandro Mayol was an Argentinian priest whom Néstor had known since 1961 when he was a minor seminarian. A composer of protest songs, Mayol also wrote reflections on social change, to which Néstor here refers.

We're ready to go. It's 7 in the morning. Today Edicita is twelve years old.[1] I remember her with special affection, since she really looks like a female replica of me. I just hope that my situation doesn't prevent her from celebrating a really happy birthday.

How are you? What I would give to be able to hear from you or see you.

Things are fine, and I think we're on the right road. The "balancing acts" of the government are a symptom of our own possibilities. They haven't said anything about the eight men who left us and were caught. I get sick every time I think of what criminal, dehumanized people are in power.

I'm thinking of Edicita again and of the last time I was in Sucre to say goodbye to my dad. He asked me to come back, and I said it was impossible. As I got into the taxi his eyes filled with tears. But let's stop the homesickness. That's masochism.

We're well rested, but a little weak. Our food has gotten very bad. During the past few days we got lucky and caught two turkeys and some wild animal, oh yes, and two monkeys. Otherwise we'd have really been hungry. Personally the hunger doesn't bother me as much as my lack of strength for walking and carrying my knapsack. We can forget our hunger, but not our legs. It will be exactly twenty days that we're in the mountains. We hope to find food for another twenty.

---

1. Edicita is Néstor's sister (see above August 2, note 1).

Sunday, August 9

My dear princess,

Yesterday I couldn't write to you because there was no time. Today before beginning the march I'll write you a short note.

There are no new developments yet, except that the government seems to have completely flipped and is still haranguing us. They don't know how to handle the case of our eight men,[1] and they're getting burnt by it.

Hunger makes us eat a lot of things that before we wouldn't even have imagined. We eat a lot of *palmito* and mushrooms. Last night we ate a really big one that looked like a yucca. Every time we do something like this, I remember you and your meals. I hope that one day we can sit together at the table like we did at our little house in Obrajes.[2] Do you remember? And cook all the sausages or pork chops we can eat. I love you, princess. How's your father? I hope he has reacted well, so that it won't be one more worry for you.

We are now on the path resting. We left at 8 A.M. and walked for a whole hour. A ten minute rest and we'll be off again.

---

1. The eight militants who were allowed by the ELN command to leave the guerrilla campaign (see above July 30 and August 2). They left the battle zone unarmed and in civilian clothes. At first au-

thorities announced they were killed in combat, but the bodies were not returned. The young guerrillas' families, university students, churchpeople, and the media accused the army of "liquidating" the unarmed non-combatants, who had gone down to surrender. After a protracted protest campaign of marches, demonstrations, and hunger strikes, the mutilated bodies were finally returned. On September 29 a large funeral procession passed through La Paz for over two hours.

2. Néstor and Cecy lived in a little mud-brick house built into the wall of the Redemptorist Parish of the Obrajes. It was in striking contrast to the comfortable parish residence and the other homes in this middle-class residential district. Néstor did two types of work here: teaching religion in the Colegio Saint Andrew's, a private school run by North American missionaries, and organizing a cooperative and forming political consciousness among young workers.

My dear love,

We just had a drink of cold chocolate, and we're ready to march again. We heard the 1 o'clock news of Radio Altiplano. It seems that another group of us has been formed in Chapare.[1] And the political situation is very good.

It's terribly cold, and we're going through very humid mountains. It's torture to sleep at night. I miss you near me, cuddled under my arm. I LOVE YOU.

Things are going fine except for certain adjustments we have to make, especially concerning people who have been stealing the food out of their comrades' knapsacks and from the community supply. I think that as soon as somebody is caught in the act, there has to be a punishment imposed for the example it gives. Perhaps execution or expulsion from the guerrillas.

Otherwise, things are fine. Still walking with strength, though I guess I've become much thinner.

---

1. Chapare is a peasant zone in the Cochabamba area. Actually, no group was formed there and the information received was probably an unverified report.

How are you, my love? Today is beautiful. We're about to enter the combat zone. We've finished the "training" and the consolidation phase of the group. Things are going smoothly. The country's political situation seems favorable to us. The thing is to break up more forcefully this tightrope balancing act.

The stars were beautiful last night, and I sat by the fire with Omar chatting and reminiscing. How pleasant it is to remember the people we love together with other people we love.

We're ready to leave, and I don't know what will happen from now on. I think tomorrow will be decisive. We drank some chocolate with milk and raw sugar. Excellent. I love you. Later I'll describe to you how I look. I have Fernández's uniform, American boots, Mario's socks and another blue pair, my blue shorts, my medal, your hair ribbon that I always carry with me, and a cap which was given to me (I lost the one I had with the little cross on it).

In my right shirt pocket is this notebook, and another one with your pictures and card. In the other is my pipe-cleaner, my pipe, a lighter, a little tobacco, a spoon, a comb, and a handkerchief. In my pants pocket (the right one) are a hundred bullets and a mosquito net. In the other pocket, a nylon string and a handkerchief. In my back pocket, the penknife hanging from my belt. I'm using my old narrow belt, which is comfortable. On top of this I wear the belt which you made me, and hanging from it from left to right are my hunting knife, my canteen and its cup, and my cartridge clips.

I look good, although I've gotten a lot thinner, something which becomes more evident with the cap, my long hair, and the "belt" of a beard around my face. The mosquito bites don't swell up any more, but they do bother me. My love, the ZK rifle which we used to keep in the house works very well, although it's a little heavy. It is one of the best in the column (as a type). Also I carry a bag on my left, and in it I keep my wool jacket and the sheepskin jacket with the money (1,000 pesos), the Psalms, the New Testament, a little coca and tobacco. The watch works perfectly—after twenty days it's only three and a half minutes slow. Everything you gave me has worked perfectly: the sewing kit, the handkerchief (which I lost), the mosquito net, the nylon bags. I have to laugh at the bags because they're all ones that either your nylon stockings or your sanitary napkins came in. Oscar made a little crucifix for me which I'll put in place as soon as I have time, probably this afternoon. My white T-shirt is now definitely black. Who knows when I'll be able to wash it. Would you believe that I don't have any blisters on my feet, but I do have two little corns on the sole of my foot. My boots are holding up, but I don't think they'll last much longer. The same for the soles of the boots.

Changing the subject, I think my presence in the column, especially in the vanguard, has been beneficial. Luis and some of our other "ex-Christian" comrades have had long conversations with me and we read the Bible together. This is good, not for proselytism (which I can't stand), but for the deepening of all that is human and vital. It is a constant and profound enrichment.

It makes me happy to realize that all my previous formation and what we learned together is helping to make us more human. I think that people see this, and I'm glad, not, I repeat, for vanity, but because it is a fundamental, inescapable service which we must do for others: to show with our "life," our example, what we believe and desire, and to have an even spirit, always the same, joyful and constructive in good times and in bad. This involves a great personal control, a basic step towards the New Man.

My adorable love, we're taking a short rest now during our long march. It's 10:40 and we're about to enter into a new stage of the guerrilla campaign. We've more or less finished our training, and now we'll see who's taken advantage of it and how. We'll be going into the Valley of Mapiri where there is a concentration of the military and peasants.

It's 11:50 and we have seen fields with a few houses. I make note of this for two reasons: First, because it means a bad beginning to the struggle. We'll have to face the peasants' inconsistency, the mountains, and the army—and all at once. Second, because there is FOOD there. It's funny how you can risk your own skin for a little corn, a pig or some other animal, yucca, bananas, a corn cake or any other little thing. The truth is that not only do we have empty stomachs, but we're weak, and that makes it really tough when we walk all day as we've usually been doing all this time . . . . It seems we have to cross the river. The army might be on the other side, or at least that seems most logical.

The men's faces are saying, "Let's stop." Since we saw the fields it's clear to everybody that a little meat with toasted corn, some fried bananas and yucca, would be a dish worthy of the Hotel Crillón.

The day after tomorrow is another anniversary, right?[1] I'll make a note of it so I won't forget. I don't

57

even want to imagine your reaction to an oversight of such magnitude.

The education of the will is really essential if you haven't been concerned with it before. This week we've had the loss of cans of preserves—condensed milk, sardines, corned beef—and the men reported them as if they had been lost or stolen. But now some have confessed their weakness to the leader. It makes me really mad to know that some bastard either by himself or with somebody else can down a can of condensed milk and deprive four or five comrades of such vital sustenance. But at least they recognized their own weakness. The punishments have been given, and we hope that these things don't happen again. Che ordered a combatant shot in the Sierra for stealing food. I'm not saying that we should take such a drastic measure, since I don't think it would be the best thing for us to do here, but I don't think the idea should be rejected if the offense is serious.

I feel well and in good spirits. My whole being, my body and soul, my mind and all that I am, have come together. I'm a leaven, but one that works steadily. At least that's the feeling I have. A great peace and a great calm fill me completely. In a vital way I'm even moving from the idea of "death" as a diminishment to the reality of "death" as fulness, and I am moving into a new dimension. I'm not seeking death, not in any way, but if it comes I'll meet it with the peace and calm that such a moment deserves, and I'll even ask them to report that I've gone to the Father, that "Come, Lord Jesus" has become real in me. If there's any shadow in all of this, it's you, your absence. I won't even say that it's physical, for I feel you within me, and this makes me a little anxious. How I'd like to share all this with you, but that time will come. I haven't lost hope.

---

1. Néstor and Cecy were married on April 14, 1968, and they commemorated this date every month.

Feast of the Virgin. I'm in an ambush. I think we're going to meet the army face to face. I'll write you later. I love you. I miss you terribly. We've already been hiding here for three hours. There's nothing abnormal, except that I'm sitting on an anthill, and they really bite.

How are things, my dear princess?

We're on the move again, knapsacks on our backs and eyes ready to spot the enemy. We've had four or five unusual days. Fantastic! We went into a small town and rested, ate, and relaxed our spirits. For the first time in my life my stomach seems like it's dancing, jumping around like a madman. Yesterday morning we left the town, and in the afternoon the planes came. It seems that they've gotten some information.

They bombed and machine-gunned quite close to where we were camped. Our group is disorganized. Morale is down, and this really worries me. It's not that anything serious has happened, but in different ways and circumstances the men are reacting aggressively, neurotically. I think that there is still a great crisis of faith among us, a crisis in the complete confidence needed in the command group and in their ability to bring this war to a successful end. I sincerely think they are capable, although there's no denying their lack of experience, especially in ordinary, everyday organizational details. But otherwise they've acted with clear vision and awareness of what they were doing and the decisions they were making.

I think that we're going to be fighting, most importantly in circumstances advantageous to us. This will either reduce certain problems or make them more serious, especially the problems of a personal nature which we have been dragging along with us. There's no doubt we still need a strong catalyst, as we would have had in Inti, Ricardo, or Pombo, or even . . . . [1] But I don't think that this has any direct relation to the degree of commitment to the revolutionary ideal that the troops demand of themselves.

I'm well and I think the others can see this, since in general they have nothing against me and I even think they respect me. If I can develop certain aspects of my life as a guerrilla, and prove I've developed by my deeds, that is, by my daily consistency, I think I'll be able to help the troops even more. I'm telling you all this because I want to continue with the kind of sincerity we've always had. To be an open book for each other. It's not that I have a great desire for promotions, but if I have something to contribute I want to do it completely. ''My eternal vocation of service'' is fashioned again here, a kind of priesthood—not ritual or externally sacramental—but very rich in concrete possibilities for love.

Omar told me that they were proposing my name as ''political officer'' in the column. This is a post which is based completely on the moral strength of the comrade who holds it. We'll see. If I get the post, I'd like to earn it either in combat or right here, after a while spent in this everyday life itself.

Guerrilla life is really a convergence point of many different dimensions and concerns. It is here that the most intimate part of each person comes into play, his metaphysical being, his personal complexity, his shortcomings and strengths, in a word, his everything.

It's exciting, but it also makes me very afraid. Because if it's not well-directed and channeled the whole thing can turn into a nuthouse.

But in and beyond all this—I LOVE YOU. Today we would be sleeping and getting ready to listen to "Agitando Pañuelos" on Radio Altiplano. Princess, it's incredible how I love you. Every time I repeat these words I find them more and more meaningful and real.

In general the people in the towns have received us well, at least they helped us in every way we asked them (always in exchange for money, of course). I wish I was in charge of this so that our conscientization efforts would have been presented as simply as possible, so that we would have a chance of coming back again, resting, leaving behind one of our sick or wounded.[2]

Men are still leaving. Yesterday another disappeared. I think we'll still have a big shake-up. I hope it finds us well prepared.

The national situation seems to be in our favor. It's a shame we don't have a good communications network. Okay, I'll leave you for now. I'm sleepy.

---

1. When the young combatants of the ELN entered the guerrilla zone, they elected "Chato" Peredo as temporary leader of the

Teoponte Campaign. Although committed to the cause, "Chato" did not possess the strong leadership qualities of a Che Guevara or his lieutenants in the Ñancahuazú campaign, among whom were Inti Peredo, eldest of the three Peredo brothers and acknowledged leader of the ELN after Che's death; Ricardo, a Chilean militant who was in charge of operations in the Cochabamba area; and Pombo, a veteran of the Cuban Sierra Maestra and survivor of Ñancahuazú who was one of Che's closest associates.

2. Successful efforts at conscientization, that is, increasing political awareness, would have led to greater understanding of and support for the guerrilla forces on the part of the people in the area.

We're ready to begin the march. Yesterday we made a trail, a long one so we'll be able to move ahead fast, even with the mule and the small bull we have with us. We don't know what to expect since the army must be trying to surround us. I just hope we meet them so we can better define our real capabilities and test our morale. And I hope we meet them under good conditions for us so that our evaluations can be clear and genuine.

I'm happy, my love. We're moving ahead with confidence on a qualitative level. Yesterday I read a little of the Apostles, their first steps, their hesitations, their discoveries, their cowardice, their confidence in the "triumph." It gave me new courage and strengthened my desire to be in the vanguard, to be a prophet of a people on the march. I especially liked the summary made by Stephen, the first Christian martyr of salvation history. It tells of the deeds of liberation, God's presence in history, and Stephen's unbreakable faith and desire to discover the Lord beyond the shadows.

We're in a dry thicket. I think we're climbing again. We'd gone down to an altitude of 400 meters and in our previous excursions we've gone up to 1500. We've already spent a month which has been really productive in experiences and contact with real situations. Maybe tomorrow or a little later on I can give you a summary and an analysis.

It's been a full month, dear princess. Yesterday we missed our chance to score our first victory. We planned an ambush, but because of our carelessness and negligence the soldiers detected the trap and didn't enter the area. Today I don't know what the command group will decide, whether to move away from the enemy or wait to strike them even though they are already alerted.

This month's experience has helped us a lot. As I told you before, we've come to know each other quite well, our weaknesses, our strengths, and our real possibilities. I think it's been a positive experience, because it's turned out well for us, both in the operations we planned and in unforeseen situations. We've noted who is strong and who is weak and who hasn't progressed. There are some who can be salvaged, but there are others who almost surely are lost. Some will leave us at any moment or will give us some kind of surprise, which I hope won't be unpleasant.

Personally I'm doing fine. I'm clear in what I'm doing, and, I think, convinced of everything that all this means. My life has a goal that is well marked out, and I feel sure that I'm heading toward it with great and complete confidence in what I'm doing, both personally and communally. As for our prospects, I think they're good. But they could be better because we are not yet fully capable of catalyzing the people. This is directly related to our internal and external effectiveness, things which have been affecting us recently.

My life with the Lord has deepened, and I think we're overcoming that "old man," who is like a snare keeping me from moving ahead and tangling up my path every time I am careless. Later I'll tell you more, but now I'm going to read Che.[1]

---

1. Ernesto Che Guevara's *Revolutionary Works* (see below October 13).

How are things going, princess? We've heard news about the "Rangers."[1] It seems that there's been some reaction throughout the country, especially in the mining sector. I expect we'll be having a skirmish with the army, and then we'll be able to define the situation a little better. The men are doing well. The cohesion of the group is coming along slowly but surely.

Today I'm going to visit Omar in the center. This morning I saw him briefly. I wonder what he'll have to say. He's a great fellow. The friendships among the men are crystallizing and becoming more solid, though it's difficult to meet someone who has the same ways as you. But we need the valuable and enriching dimensions of a friendship on a practical level: to save extra food, to share personal things, to profit mutually from the strengths and best qualities each one has to offer. Time and the greater openness it brings will teach me this.

I'm beginning to stink again. I hope I have a chance to take a bath and change my underwear. My boots are still holding up. I just hope they last another month because they're very comfortable.

I've been thinking about our trip to Sucre and the meals we ate there. We've been eating some delicious corn and banana cakes, two or three helpings in the morning and another two or three at night. But still I always feel hungry. Hunger is a constant in this life. The food does keep us going though.

How are things with Jaime, Carmen, and the children?[2] I hope their Marxism is working out well. I miss all of you. The day will come when we'll all be together again. There are some here who have asked me for the New Testament and the Psalms, and they've been reading them. I think it helps. Okay, I'm sending you a superloving kiss.

---

1. The Bolivian Rangers were army troopers especially trained by U.S. experts in counter-insurgency warfare, based at the Southern Command headquarters in the Panama Canal Zone. The Rangers had a reputation for their repressive capacity, and their effectiveness was proven by the successful operations that led to the capture and death of Che Guevara. It was also the Rangers who claimed responsibility for the operations which nearly wiped out the ELN guerrillas in the Teoponte Campaign.

2. Néstor's brother Jaime is married to Carmen, a Spaniard and a convinced Marxist (see above August 2, note 1). They have no children; the "children" here are their political friends, as companions sharing the same vision and ideology were sometimes affectionately referred to in this way.

I'll begin again with another superloving kiss. I haven't been writing because our marches have been irregular. Today I'm writing from the top of a very high mountain range, one of the highest in this area. We're going down into a big valley where we'll do some "dirty deeds." But I think it will also be the beginning of our losses. I hope not. There's a large population here, and so there are plenty of army soldiers. It seems that they've announced the names of the eight of our group who were killed. We'll listen to the 1 o'clock news.

Things are going well and the days are flying by. I feel perfectly and fully well. If we succeed according to our plan, the country will have some heroic and glorious moments. I just hope that everything turns out without unexpected factors going against us. The troops are getting more confident and the basic difficulties are beginning to disappear. One more left us, a lazy, good-for-nothing bum. So much the better. I just hope that the army hasn't captured him, because they'll really give him a hard time. Yesterday I heard some news on Radio Fides[1] about the cement factory.[2] It made me really glad. If my father is still in that post, he'll have a lot of work to do.

How I miss your toasted butter bread. I've learned to appreciate it here in all its "breadth and depth." I love you and it's growing by the minute. I'm glad when the days fly by so fast, because we'll be together again that much sooner. What a day that will be! I think it will be one of the greatest of my life, that day and the day of our victory. Do you remember the movie we saw about Isadora and her dance with the Russian Army? And the pork dinner we had at the Automobile Club? And the last meals we had at Mario's place and the ham you cooked? So many happy things brought us together during those last days. I have to leave you for now.

It's rained a lot and I've slept only a little because I had to stay up the night before last to prepare the food for the group. We killed a young bull which we bought in the town, and this gave us between a quarter and a half kilo of roasted meat for each of us during the last few days. This is all the food we have, and we have to ration it carefully. It has to last till this afternoon, because we don't want to make another fire. Last night I cut it into little pieces and used the pepper you had put with the salt. I ate like we did in the Daiquiri[3]—it was even better. Quirito and Oscar and I were reminiscing about the great meals at the house in Sopocachi[4] and all the great things we had to leave behind when we set out. I love you. Ciao.

---

1. An independent, Jesuit-operated radio station in La Paz, known for its objective news analysis and commentaries.

2. Néstor's father, a retired Brigadier General of the Bolivian

71

armed forces, was president of the Board of Directors of the cement factory in Sucre.

3. A La Paz restaurant known for its *parrilladas* (roasted beef).

4. Sopocachi is the residential neighborhood where the school directed by Cecy's mother was located. After some time in Obrajes (see above August 9, note 2), Néstor and Cecy transferred to Sopocachi, building a similar makeshift home. This was their last home before Néstor left for Teoponte.

My dear princess: It's been raining since dawn and it's already 10:30 A.M. Yesterday we crossed a river. We waded through and then we had a really long and tough march. The climb was like the one we had a while back.

We ate the mule we had with us. Out here you learn to eat everything. The beast was pretty good, even though it made my stomach play tricks. Each of us had a ration of corn and pumpkin, and also some bananas. I'm rationing it for myself so that I don't eat it all at once. It has to last a few days.

We're in the belly of the monster. The planes fly right over our heads as they take off from a nearby airport.

Yesterday Radio Fides read a letter or message of mine from the guerrilla zone to my folks. I don't know if it's the one I wrote from home the night before I left or if it's a paragraph I wrote to Archbishop Manrique.[1] Anyway, if it was the second, it means the message got there. So I'm getting famous and you're getting jealous. Yesterday they read Choquito's letter on Radio Altiplano. It was really beautiful. What a tragic end for someone with such a noble spirit.

Things are going well. You'll be hearing from us during these coming days.

1. Archbishop Jorge Manrique of La Paz was head of the commission formed to mediate between the government and the ELN guerrillas. Because of the high-handed attitude of the military, the archbishop resigned from the commission, but on his own continued looking for more direct and personal means to contact the guerrillas. It was on the initiative of the archbishop that a group headed by Fr. Jaime Zalles was formed. Fr. Zalles was later able to rescue six of the Teoponte survivors in a town near Tipuani.

My adorable love: The last few days have been beautiful and, I think, profitable in every way. We have gone deeply into populated areas and this brings us into contact with the peasant-army.[1]

We bought a huge pig and got lard from it. We each had two big plates of crackling fried in boiling lard, plus four big bananas. We also got enough corn for two or three days and three kilos of rice. I think from now on food won't be a problem, although we'll always have to keep some in reserve just in case. Another comrade and I were assigned to cook the pig and the bananas. I think they turned out well. We did the best we could with everything. I think the "dance" is beginning. The army isn't right on top of us yet, but it will be soon. It's been raining and the visibility is low. That's to our advantage.

I hope the letter read on Radio Fides made you happy. What I would give to hear from you. We are being purified. Combat will purge us even more. Out of this experience that select group will be drawn which will bring the people to the happiness they so rightly deserve. This is the result of a long and constant faithfulness to the revolutionary ideal incarnated in the life of the guerrilla.

I'll leave you for now. I don't even have to tell you I

want your head on my shoulder—to kiss you in my dreams.

———

1. The peasant-army was organized by General René Barrientos to combat the guerrillas and the striking miners. It was formed at the suggestion of the U.S. Counter-Insurgency Forces.

My dear princess: Today I'm writing under pretty heavy pressure. Yesterday we received a severe blow which hurt us a lot and weakened the men's morale. Those who haven't come back include Condorito, Pablo, and Gregorio. I hate to say it, but I think their fates are sealed. There were many reasons for this disaster. The main ones are (1) we didn't have sufficient mobility because of one of the wounded men; (2) we were completely careless concerning the enemy and underestimated their strength; (3) the command group lacked the experience necessary to foresee and decide certain things in time.

Because of this I've been thinking that life is really given to us from moment to moment. The Gospel command becomes totally clear and relevant under these circumstances. At any moment, "you can go." If you're wounded they'll have to leave you behind in as safe a place as possible, but then the army is liable to find you and finish you off. But we have to remember that the fate of the column and the revolution itself cannot depend on the life of any one of us, no matter how valuable he may be. We have to understand this very clearly so we don't distort the depth of this real fact.

In spite of all this I have not become discouraged. Today I know more realistically what's happening in the history of my life and what I've committed myself to. The ideological dimension takes on all its meaning here, just as the evangelical dimension does. The Good News comes to life when you live it, and you really live it here.

I hope that later we'll be able to recuperate with a good offensive—that this is the beginning of a real vanguard of liberation. It's a shame we can't accomplish all this overnight and without such bitter moments.

I love you much more intensely for what you are and what you mean to me. All that we have been through and dreamed together, today I feel it as strongly as the smell of mint or an orange tree.

I don't know. I don't think I'm going to die. I have that feeling. But if I die I want my death to be full of meaning, to create waves of repercussion and reach other ''receptive ears'' who will struggle for the happiness of man.[1] I'm conscious of this and I am convinced we will achieve it.

We're going to restructure our column to fill up the vacancies and replace some of the men. I don't know if they'll replace me. I think I'll find out today. Once again I want to offer all that I am and all that I am trying to become to the service of this group. I leave you for now. I love you with all my heart.

1. A reference to Che Guevara's famous "Message to the Tricontinental," which concludes, "Wherever death may suprise us, let it be welcome, provided that this, our battle cry, may have reached some receptive ear and another hand may be extended to wield our weapons and other men be ready to intone the funeral dirge with the staccato singing of the machine-guns and new battle cries of war and victory" (*Venceremos! The Speeches and Writings of Che Guevara*, ed. John Gerassi [New York: Macmillan, 1968], p. 424).

My adorable love: It's 2:30 P.M. and we're resting. We've been marching in horrible weather—raining and very cold. Today during the march one of the men came close to a serious accident. It would have been fatal, especially now when we're trying to move ahead and take the initiative against the government.

Yesterday I was named political officer of the column. I took over from Felipe. You can imagine the responsibility they've put on my shoulders and what it means in my life. Like I said before, I just hope I can contribute my best to the men, especially by example. Things are going well. I think we've about reached the peak of our fighting form.

Last night I was listening to a commentary on Radio Fides about us. I wonder what they'll be saying about us when we settle accounts with the system through the army?

This is a specific option and a hard life, a very hard life. We must overcome ourselves, the enemy, and the forces of nature, with its hunger, its thirst, its rain, its terrain, its bullets, its selfishness . . . .

We'll come out ahead, I'm sure, especially in those regions which lie ahead of us where we can operate with more security and impact.

I'll be thinking of you, tomorrow especially. I love you and I need you, but I know you are truly by my side. I leave you for now. I'll continue later.

My adorable love: Forgive me for not writing for the last few days. We have had some very difficult moments and the days have been very full. We ran into a series of rough situations—the division of the column into two groups, two clashes with the army, men killed—all with a result that is encouraging and difficult at the same time. Encouraging because in general we are still a compact and dedicated group, although fewer in number. Painful, because we've lost contact with a part of our column which has some very valuable men in it. Painful too because of the loss of priceless men like Gregorio, Condorito, Pablo, and maybe others. It's true that we're getting combat experience, but the price is high. Our alternative, beyond the basic option of struggle to Victory or Death, is to survive as well as we can to give continuity to the struggle and wait for reinforcements. We had foreseen these problems, so I hope we don't have very serious setbacks.

I'm joining the command group as political officer. The group includes Chato, Omar, Dante (the peasant), and Gastón. It's a well-knit group, and we get along very well. Last night Chato and the rest of us made an analysis of the situation and I think things are clearly settled. Hard days are ahead, intense days. News from the cities is encouraging. The massacre at Tupiza,[1] the hunger strike at the University,[2] the support of the

COB,[3] etc. I think if we continue with our usual hit and run tactics we can create a climate of conflict which will make conditions clearly favorable to us within a short time.

I have thought about you a lot, especially during these rough and difficult days we've been through. All of us know how crucial the situation is and how hard the time ahead will be. But our spirit and morale are enough to overcome any difficulty, no matter how great. I imagine the army will use everything they have against us, trying to wipe us out as quickly as they can. But as I said before, I think enough of us will survive to carry on the struggle, keeping alive this "little candle" which we have lit and which continues to burn.

I'll leave you for now. We're moving ahead.

---

1. A demonstration organized by university students in Tupiza, Potosí, evolved into a violent confrontation between students and police, in which two students were killed and fourteen others wounded. The march had been organized to support the families of the eight ex-university leaders who had left the guerrilla ranks, been captured alive, and then killed by the military.

2. The University of San Andrés in La Paz. University students, churchpeople, media representatives, and families of the slain guerrillas (see note 1 above) had organized hunger strikes and protest marches in demonstration of their solidarity with the men in the Teoponte Campaign. One of their main demands was the return of the bodies of the eight men. They roundly denounced the repressive measures of the army which did not respect the lives of their prisoners of war. When the government finally returned the bodies, examination of the remains clearly indicated that the group had been machine-gunned.

3. The COB was the powerful tin miners' union, the *Central Obrera Boliviana* (Bolivian Workers' Organization). After an emergency meeting, the group declared their moral and material support for the relatives of the dead guerrillas who were carrying out the hunger strike. Union leaders joined the strike, a move of great political significance.

My love: We have come to a stop in our march. We heard some shots to our left, but we don't know exactly where they came from.

I've been with you constantly. These days have been very intense, charged with meaning. They might be our last—or the first of our victory. I think more of the second possiblility because, analyzing things coldly, I think we still have good chances. In the midst of our group we have an excellent "family" life. In Black Omar especially I've found a brother more than a comrade. This reassures me and gives me tremendous confidence. The political situation is very good, but we're a little tied up by our own situation.

Allende won in Chile, and this opens up great possibilities. If in Latin America an entire people is capable of choosing socialism, it means that the conditions are established—no doubt about it.

I LOVE YOU. I'll write again soon.

My love: We find ourselves in an interesting situation. There are twenty-three of us left. At last we're ready for ANYTHING. We have a tight-knit column. Yesterday we had our first political session, with a talk, an analysis of the situation, and some readings. I directed it, my debut as political officer. It was very profitable, and we came to some clear-cut conclusions on our goals. There were contributions from comrades like Kolla, peasants who gave their points of view on rural conditions and the reactions of the people who work in the fields. Others contributed in the same way, and Chato summarized the discussion. It was a good start.

Things are going well in the midst of the drama of the moment. On the one hand, we know what we have created as catalysts within the national situation. On the other hand, we also know how tough a blow our physical annihilation would be to the cause and how much of the effort would collapse with our defeat.

My own life is going very well. I was happy to find a New Testament which one of the men was carrying with him. It's like gold. As a group we have reached a certain level of intimacy. Besides having a good friend in Black Omar, there are two others from Tarija, Jesús and the Chapaco Adrián. There's also the old group of priceless friends like Quiridito, Rogelio, Omar, and the others.

Something good will come out of this, something truly good that will change the future history of this country.

I miss you terribly. How I wish we could live through this more closely together so we could grow in it, even though what you are doing is the same thing.

My dear Lord: It's been a long time since I've written. Today I really feel the need of you and your presence. Maybe it's because of the nearness of death or the relative failure of our struggle. You know I've always tried to be faithful to you in every way, consistent with the fulness of my being. That's why I'm here. I understand love as an urgent demand to solve the problem of the other—where you are.

I left what I had and I came. Maybe today is my Holy Thursday and tonight will be my Good Friday. Into your hands I surrender completely all that I am with a trust having no limits, because I love you. What hurts me most is perhaps leaving behind those I love the most—Cecy and my family—and also not being able to experience the triumph of the people, their liberation.

We are a group filled with authentic humanity, "Christian" humanity. This, I think, is enough to move history ahead. This encourages me. I love you, and I give to you all that I am and all that we are, without measure—because you are my Father.

Nobody's death is useless if his life has been filled with meaning, and I believe ours has been.

Ciao, Lord, perhaps until we meet in your heaven, that new land that we yearn for so much.

My dear love: Just a few lines for you. I don't have the energy for any more. I have been tremendously happy with you. It hurts me deeply to leave you alone, but if I must, I will. I'm here till the end, which is Victory or Death.

I love you. I give you all that I am, all that I can, with all the strength I have. I'll see you soon—either here or there. I'm giving you a big kiss and protecting you in my arms.

October 2

My dear princess: I haven't written for many days
because I just haven't had the strength. Yesterday I was
thinking a lot about everything that is OURS.

We are undergoing extremely difficult and dis-
couraging moments.

My body is broken, but my spirit is whole. I want to
give myself to you, first of all, and then to others. I love
you with all my strength and with all that I am able, for
you are the incarnation of my life, my struggle, and my
dreams.

It will be difficult for us to be together on the 9th.
Maybe the 29th or at Christmas.[1] But I'm confident that
we will be together.

We're a small group. It's good to be with comrades
who are also friends or relatives. It gives me a lot of
peace. At times like these it's hard not to despair. It's
trust in the Lord Jesus that gives me the courage to go
on till the end.

We have lost the battle, at least this one, and there's
nothing that can be done. We'll have to recoup our
resources and decide clearly and realistically what we
can do in the future. We'll see.

I only hope that we'll see each other on this side of
death, even though after death our reunion would be

complete and full of happiness. I believe in this and it comforts me.

I hope to be with you soon, to have long talks, to look at each other, to bring a little Paz into this world who will fill our days with joy, and to move ahead. I'm afraid something's happened to you, but I hope you're okay.

I'll leave you now. As always paper isn't enough for what I want to say. I'm no good at writing. I can hardly express myself. I'm thinking of the folks, my brothers and sisters. I'll be hugging them soon. More than anything else I want to eat and eat and eat the first few days. We haven't had anything for a month except for a little bite of whatever we could find here or there. I love you and I want you to understand this perfectly. I love you more than anything and I love you completely . . . .

----

1. October 9 is Néstor's birthday; October 29 is Cecy's birthday.

ALBERTO'S CONTINUATION
OF THE JOURNAL

Seeing that Néstor was no longer able to write in his journal, a Chilean companion in the Teoponte Campaign, José Miguel Celis González ("Alberto"), took up the task of relating the account of his last days and death.

We've divided the column of Omar, Gastón, Jesús, Santiago, Rogelio, Quiro, Francisco, and I. We are staying by the bank of a river called Mariapo in a little hut presumably built by a peasant or a hunter. Francisco, Quiro, and I are staying behind in the hut. At 11 o'clock Omar, Gastón, Rogelio, Jesús, and Santiago are leaving. They promised to come back and get us in three days and bring us some food.

The three of us have stayed behind. Francisco is so weak that he can hardly take care of his basic needs by himself. Quiro could do a little more, but he doesn't so he won't get any weaker. I'm in better shape than my two comrades, so I've taken charge of the situation, taking care of fetching firewood and water and cooking lard with salt which the other men left behind. There is enough for a quarter of a spoonful a day.

I got up at about 7 this morning and fixed breakfast. Francisco had a hard time eating. I had to help him. He couldn't even get up to urinate, so we found a can in the hut that he used. Francisco asked me if we could talk about his wife and of our chances of getting out of this—which are remote—and also a little about my own life. Quiro remained silent. He doesn't want to die. All I do is fetch firewood and water.

I woke up at 5 this morning. Francisco woke up at 5:30. He spoke to Quiro and told him to listen to the noises, which he said were from a pig. He asked Quiro to kill it, to shoot it. Quiro told him to shut up and not to bother him and to let him sleep. I told Francisco that there wasn't any pig.

He said to me, "Albertito, is it true that my cousin's coming October 9th?"

"Yes. He's coming and he's going to bring food."

"I'd like to be with Cecy on my birthday and eat the noodles she cooks. My poor Cecy. I love her so much."

It's 7 in the morning. I fixed breakfast and offered some to Francisco, but he was already speaking very slowly and he said to me, "Good buddy, I can't."

I told Quiro to eat breakfast with me so that afterwards he could help me feed Francisco. Then Quiro helped me sit him up, but he couldn't even open his mouth. I fed him his breakfast with a spoon and we laid him down very slowly. He told me he had to pee, but he couldn't even open his fly so I had to do it for him. I helped him get on his back. Then he didn't say anything else. Quiro was lying down beside him, and I was lying in a hammock.

I slept till 11:30. Quiro was awake, but with his eyes closed. At 12 noon Quiro said very sadly, "Alberto, Francisco's dead."

"No!" I cried. I got out of my hammock.

Quiro took his pulse and put his ear on his heart. "He's dead," Quiro said with tears in his eyes, "and it's 12 o'clock, the same hour and the same day that Ernesto Che Guevara died." Quiro cried very bitterly and he made me cry.

I thought of our duty to the body of our Christian comrade, and we decided to read a part of the New Testament that spoke about death. Quiro and I read and reflected for about a quarter of an hour.

Then Quiro and I looked at each other. We realized that only the two of us were left. Tomorrow or the day after one of us would go too—either him or me. We talked about the chances of surviving. There weren't any.

Last night I thought it would be good to move Francisco's body, because it was very close to the fire; also, so that Quiro could move into Francisco's place. It was hard to convince him because he didn't have the strength to move and help me. Fransisco was very heavy, but we made the switch and then I got firewood and water. I tried to find some wild fruit, but there wasn't any. I thought of knocking down a palm tree with the grenades we had left, but it wasn't possible. Quiro is desperate. He doesn't want to die. He claims there's a chance we won't die and says we should send messages in medicine bottles down the Mariapo River. I told him, "Okay. We'll send the first one out tomorrow at 5."

"All right," he said. "Tomorrow at five."

Quiro has had it. We ran out of lard. Now we just have salt and water. I'm afraid of being left alone. I went down to the river to brush my teeth. I was in the river and I heard a shot. I thought it was the army. I came back up to the hut and saw blood running down Quiro's face, and I asked him what happened.

"Brother, please, if I faint, give me a shot."

"What should I do, Quiro?"

Quiro said that there were injections for killing pain in Francisco's knapsack.

"But I don't know how to do it!"

"Just stick it in," he said.

I gave him the injection. He calmed down and I asked him to explain the gunshot to me. He said, "I wanted to shoot a bird, but my Mauser rifle went off accidentally and the shot hit me in the jaw. What makes it worse is that if I get out of this I'm going to look like a monster." Poor Quiro.

Francisco's body is decomposing. It has a lot of insects on it. I think I'll have to bury the body. I talked with Quiro. We discussed whether we should bury it or not. We don't have anything to do it with. We only have the knife Gastón left behind.

I wrapped Francisco's body in a hammock and sewed it up like a mummy. I tied a rope to it and then I went down to the river. I pulled on the rope and the body rolled until it hit a tree trunk. I got it away from the trunk and pulled again until I got down to the river bank. I think the body burst. The hammock was wet and green. I left it there and came back to my hammock worn out from the work.

Even though the body is far away (50 meters), the smell is so strong I can't sleep. I think I'm going to try to cross the river.

I picked up the rope, got into the water, and pulled. The body floated, but it quickly got away from me into the middle of the river. It was very heavy. I fell in the water and the current dragged the body and me along. I had to let go. It was terrible. I didn't mean to. The current carried it away. I told Quiro. He just shook his head.

It's good to prepare for death. We depend on miracles and miracles are relative. Quiro is reading Francisco's diary. In his knapsack Francisco had the *Revolutionary Works* of Ernesto Che Guevara. Inside the cover it said, "To be a revolutionary we have to discover Christ, and once we discover Christ we will be revolutionaries."

He also had a New Testament, which was mine, his diary, a notebook, pictures of his wife and a friend. I think I should wrap them up in plastic so they don't get ruined. Someday somebody will find these things, and they'll know who they belong to. It's terrible to die of hunger. We would have liked to die fighting or in combat like Casiano[1] and the other comrades.

---

1. "Casiano" was the battle-name of Benjo Cruz, a well-known folk and protest singer, who left his career to join the guerrilla column. He was considered one of the best combatants, although he had little military preparation. He was wounded, captured alive, tied to a tree, told to sing and machine-gunned to death.

I began to go down at 9 A.M. I met a boy on the road, together with the boy who had left me waiting the day before. We greeted each other and they took me to my friends. When I got there it was a moving scene. My comrades were very thin and weak and could hardly move. We greeted each other.

Omar asked me, "How could Francisco have been wounded?" He had bad information. I told him Francisco had died. He was stunned by the news and his face grew very sad. Poor Omar. He was Francisco's cousin. I gave him a full report after lunch, and turned over all Francisco's belongings to him.

Omar began to read Francisco's diary.

OMAR'S FINAL NOTE

On the last page of Francisco's campaign journal,
Omar, the Marxist leader of the small surviving group
and Francisco's cousin, briefly noted:

Néstor Paz Zamora, "Francisco,"
died on October 8th at 12 noon.
Cousin: You have given me the greatest lesson
of love for mankind.
Thank you.
Omar.

Lorena, October 19, 1970

DATE DUE

MY 1			